Answers to Job Interview Questions

Learn How to Respond
When It Really Matters
With Answers to Job
Interview Questions

Some surveys have shown that there are more than 90 questions that could be asked during a job interview. Of these, 15 in particular are asked most frequently during an extended interview (more than 20 minutes) for a regular work-a-day job.

Always remember that in a job interview, it is not just what you say, but how you say it that really counts. Your choice of words is powerful, and can move job interviewers to a more positive impression by how you say what you say. Here, in no particular order, are the answers to the 15 most frequently asked questions during a job interview:

1) Which position are you most interested in?

When you are responding to an advertisement, the company will likely know the position for which you have applied. Many times companies key their advertisements so, when they are advertising for more than one position, they can identify the position for which you have applied. Most public service organizations will have a specific job number with the job announcement.

However, no matter what position for which you may have applied, many companies have more than one position to offer, and the interviewer is probably going to consider you for any position available based on your submitted resume and interview performance.

Key to answering this question is to realize that different companies and organizations may call essentially the same positions by different job titles; therefore, it is best if you answer the kind of function you are interested in performing rather than a specific job title.

Hence, say "I am interested in accounting," or "I am good at accounting," rather than "I am interested in the Junior Accountant position."

2) Are you looking for full-time or part-time work?

When you are dealing with a large business or public service corporation, chances are the position is full-time, and you should be prepared to accept full-time employment.

However, when you are trying to get your foot in the door, it is well to remember that many companies hire full-time employees from their part-time and temporary help. This makes sense from a business standpoint in that they are then hiring a person they have had an opportunity to observe on the job.

When you are considering a public service position (working for the federal, state or local governmental entities, for example), it generally makes sense to accept any position as long as two factors are present:

1) That it is a full-time permanent position, and

2) You are entitled to all the normal benefits.

Most public service positions offer opportunities for advancement within the organization, and some even allow you to apply, take tests and interview for positions during your normal working hours.

You can, in some cases, look for a better job and get paid for looking during your normal working hours.

This is indeed a good deal for the employee; most private businesses would not tolerate this action and, quite frankly, some would find a "legitimate reason" to fire you if they thought you were looking.

3) Are you willing to travel or relocate (go where the company sends you)?

Decide which is more important to you: where you live, or whether you want the position, and answer accordingly. You may be willing to travel (this could be anything from commuting to another city to work to being out of town two weeks every month), but not willing to relocate.

When you are married and earn a secondary income for your family, relocating is not always practical.

4) How much money do you want to earn?

Rather than trying to figure out what they are willing to pay, or revealing what you are willing to settle for (both very risky at best), say this: "What is your salary range for this position?" This tells them nothing, puts the ball back in their court, and you remain a class act.

Another possible answer: "While the salary I would receive is certainly a consideration, I am far more interested in a position that uses performance to determine promotion and compensation. I am interested in being rewarded for my production for the company, thereby proving my value to the company."

Do ask about benefits if the interviewer does not detail the company benefit package, as the benefit package can add substantially to your salary base. In some cases the benefit package can add 30% to your salary.

5) When can you start work?

The answer is immediately when you are not working, or two weeks—or whatever the notice of termination time is—when you are working. When you are employed and can begin work immediately, your potential employer might wonder if you would quit on them without notice.

6) How long do you expect to work?

Use "As long as it is mutually beneficial for both of us." When you are the spouse of a career military person, the interviewer may want to know how long you will be around (that is, your spouse's rotation date). That is why it is best to use the suggested answer. After all, you can not predict everything that might happen. Many military families have found this out when a war or military action started.

7) Why are you interested in this position?

When you are an accountant and you are applying at an accounting firm, it is pretty obvious why you are interested; you are interested in using your acquired education, skills, and knowledge in your career field.

However, maybe the position is a cashier for a store and you just want a job; you do not have a brilliant answer to offer. Not to worry. Do not discount very basic answers such as "I need to earn money to support myself and/or my family," or "I want more out of life, and I need to work if I am going to have a better lifestyle for my family."

Employers like employees who need to work; such employees are more apt to be dependable, responsible and productive.

8) Why do you want to work for us?

Here you should be specific in your answer. There may be thousands of accounting firms with positions to offer, but it is now a question of "why us"?

Research the firm as best you can. Phone book ads often contain great information, such as how long a firm has been in business, what it specializes in, who are the key members of the firm, and whom they hope to serve. Depending upon what you learn at the library, and from other local sources, possible answers might be:

"You have an expanding firm, and I believe there will be opportunities for me to prove myself and grow with you," or

"Your firm is one of the oldest and most respected in our community, and I want to learn from, and be associated with one of the best," or

"I believe you will reward people according to their value to the firm, and I am willing to prove my value to you," or finally

"Your specialty happens to be my area of career interest."

9) Why should we hire you?

Here you must be straightforward and confident about your ability and what you have to offer. Say, "I believe I am qualified and can do the job."

Amplify this answer by stressing your strong points, such as your appropriate education, specialized training, proven experience, skills and abilities.

Do not say you can do any job. You do not know that for a fact, and, more important, the person interviewing you—no matter how good you look on paper or act in person—does not really know if you can do it either until you start having to perform on the job.

This is why you should qualify your answers with "I believe . . . ," or "Based on my performance in similar positions in the past, I have no reason to think I will not be able to do the job for you."

10) What are your strengths and weaknesses?

Good strengths include some very basic character traits, such as determination, honesty, responsibility, dependability, inquisitiveness, willingness to learn, openness to new ideas, stability, and humor. Pick traits that you are confident and comfortable with.

In approaching the question of your weaknesses, rule one is to have some. The worst answer you could give is "I do not have any weaknesses." We all have weaknesses, and if we are unwilling to talk about them, it is a big red flag that there are some definite personality problems.

Never let your lack of confidence, or overdeveloped ego, prevent you from showing your weaknesses. Handle the challenge by taking your weaknesses (whatever they may be) and turning them into strengths. If you are a workaholic, say "Sometimes I do not know when to stop working on a project. I can get so involved I may work 16 hours straight. This may upset other employees who quit at the normal time."

11) What are your career goals?

Your objectives or goals are very important. You do not want to be a wandering generality; you want to be a meaningful specific.

Employers want to know if you have thought about your future, and have a plan to get where you want to go. You should have both short and long range goals. A good short range goal might be to secure a position in your career field, develop more experience in an area of interest, or position yourself with a firm or organization that is growing.

Long range goals require you to picture yourself, and where you would like to be, 10 or 20 years from now.

12) Why did you leave your last position?

This question can be asked because they are testing your reaction, or if your resume gives the impression you have been "job-hopping". If there was a problem with leaving your last position (you were fired, encountered a personality conflict, or got mad and quit), be careful not to speak ill of the position you held, the organization you held it with, or members of the organization. Put downs score no points and reflect poorly on you, regardless of the challenges you may have had.

Good reasons to leave jobs are: 1) an opportunity for advancement, 2) an opportunity to make more money, 3) an opportunity to secure more or better benefits, 4) to gain more job satisfaction, 5) a better career opportunity, 6) a more challenging position, or 7) an opportunity to work with better people.

While all of these are legitimate reasons, none of them is the best answer to the question. It is best to simply say, "I am looking for a better opportunity." The better opportunity could be any of the above seven answers without actually saying so.

13) Do you have references?

It is not a good idea to give references at the resume stage. References are far more appropriate at the interview stage, and even then, do not give references unless they ask for them. When and if they ask, always have them available at the interview.

The reason you do not want to be giving references at the resume stage is that, if they can read your resume and check your references and—on that basis—make a decision not to interview or hire you, you have done yourself a real disservice. You want to get in front of people (secure interviews). Give them the resume, but not the references unless they ask for them.

Most prospects give names, addresses and phone numbers for references when asked. It is better not to do this. It inconveniences the interviewer in that they have to call to get the reference. And while you think you know what someone may say about you, the fact is, you do not.

The references being called may not be available, or may be on vacation. They may have left the firm, been fired or laid off since you last checked their availability.

Therefore, it is best to use written references only. Have the person put the written reference about you on the company's or organization's letterhead so it looks official, and have them sign it. If the person giving the reference will not put it on company letterhead because it is against company policy, then have them use a plain sheet of paper. They can still use their name, company position, and company name at the bottom of the letter.

Usually, written references are taken at face value. Oftentimes, with a written reference, a call is made only to verify employment.

Many candidates think that written references have to come from the big boss, or their immediate supervisor. You have other options if your boss or supervisor will not do it for you, or if you would not want them to do it for you.

When you have little work experience and have volunteered at your church, have your priest or pastor write a reference attesting to your character, ambition, dependability and productivity.

When you have worked with key employees, supervisors or managers of other companies, ask them to write you a reference attesting to your professionalism and ability to work with people.

When you have worked closely with vendors, suppliers, or their sales representatives, ask them to write you a letter of reference. You could even have another person holding the same position at another company, who you have worked with, write you a reference.

Ask a lot of people to write references because many of them will agree to do it and be happy to do it, but, unfortunately, you are not on the top of their priority list. You can be forgotten despite their good intentions to help you. Ask a lot of people and realize that for every 10 people you ask who are willing to do it and happy to do it, you will be doing very well to get 1 or 2 to actually do it.

And, when all else fails, remember that any written job evaluations you have can also be used as references until you can secure written references. You do not need a lot of references. Two or three are adequate, and they can be personal (about you) as well as professional (about the job you do).

14) Do you have any questions?

It is very important that you have questions at the interview. Any question you ask shows an indicated interest, or genuine concern on your part.

When any of the basic questions about the job have not been covered in the interview, this is a good time to ask about salary, benefits, what is expected, how you will be evaluated, and the opportunities for advancement. Other good questions include:

"Is your company or organization growing?" (Growing organizations create jobs and promotions.)

"What happened to the last person who held the position?" (Maybe they were not fired or incompetent. Maybe the company offered no advancement or salary increases, encouraged lousy working conditions, or refused to get rid of an incompetent boss.)

"How committed are you to research and development?" (Companies that invest in their future plan to be successful, profitable, and on the cutting edge of what is happening in their industry.)

"How fast can people who perform be promoted?" (You want to know that, when you produce, you will be compensated for your effort rather than draw the same salary as another employee who produces far less by comparison.)

"Is this company family owned and operated?" (When it is, you can forget getting anywhere very fast; all of the relatives will get the positions, and this will happen in many cases whether the relatives are competent or not.)

"Is there any possibility of an equity interest in the future?" (Buying in, even on a little scale, can be lucrative. More than one employee has become a millionaire by taking advantage of stock options. Look at the fortunes people made when they hooked up with Microsoft, when the software giant grew so rapidly.)

15) What would you do if . . . ? This question about imagined situations is usually posed to evaluate your reaction and judgment about decision-making matters involving the position.

The answer here is to remember that the quality of your solution is not nearly as important as your attitude and approach toward the solution.

10

Your first answer should be that the situation is probably not new, and your first move would be consult your superior who has more knowledge and experience in dealing with the problem, or you would ask others who have likely encountered the situation how they resolved the problem.

Then, be sure to qualify your answer, whatever it may be. Say "I might consider . . .," rather than "I would . . ." Always strive to be calm and rational in your approach, and certainly be open to receiving more information upon which to base a decision, or take an action.

Remember, too, that some problems will resolve themselves if you do not rush to judgment too quickly. Sometimes responding quickly actually adds to the problem or challenge. Even consultants oftentimes suggest the right answer to the wrong problem. Consultants can be quick to tell you the answer to your problem when they have not even identified the actual problem, but thought they did.

The bottom line here is to know that the more information you have, and the better it is, the more likely you are to make an intelligent decision.

This ends the answers to the 15 most frequently asked questions during a job interview, and almost begs the question: What do employers really want when hiring? The answer may surprise you.

Most potential employees are told that employers are looking for someone with a degree and hands-on skills.

While this is true in many cases, you should know that employers are also looking for someone who can do the job.

This is why they are not necessarily looking for someone with only education, experience and knowledge, as important as these three attributes may be.

Some employers will not hold it against you if you do not have education, experience, knowledge or obvious ability going for you.

For some prospects, the ego is so well developed that an employer cannot teach them anything because they already know everything.

The ego, in this case, becomes a barrier to learning.

11

It is really helpful to be an open, willing spirit without all the answers; and this applies whether you have education, experience, knowledge and ability, or you do not.

While employers may not hold it against you if you do not have education, experience and knowledge, they will hold it very much against you if you have a poor personality and cannot get along (work) with people. Remember that attitude drives personality. A person with a good attitude generally has a good personality. A person with a bad attitude generally has a bad personality.

In other words, the single biggest thing you have going for yourself is people skills. People skills are more important in the long run than education, experience, knowledge, talent and intelligence.

Some clients feel people skills are an option. They are not an option; they are mandatory if you expect to get ahead in this world.

When you greet customers or fellow employees, the last thing a business or organization can afford is for you to cost them customers, or the support of other employees because you are a negative person who cannot get along or work with other people.

Believe it or not, the two most important qualities you have going for you are 1) Your personality, which is driven by your attitude, and 2) Your ability to deal with people effectively.

Therefore, it makes all kinds of sense to sell yourself first in an interview before you sell your education, experience, knowledge or special abilities. It is vital in an interview to establish a high likeability factor, without it, you may not get an offer, no matter what qualifications you are bringing to the position.

If you do no more than learn how to smile, be enthusiastic, and act interested in people, it may well take you farther than the knowledge gained by an expensive college education combined with a bad attitude.

About the Author: Ed Bagley is a Professional Writer, Author, Ghostwriter and Personal Marketing Specialist. He has helped 5,400+ clients get jobs during a 25-year career.

A free bonus for you:

5 Power Secrets
Of Getting Hired
In Today's Economy

Ed Bagley

5 Power Secrets
Of Getting Hired
In Today's Economy

Ed Bagley

First Printing – 1998
Second Printing – 2006 (Revised)
Email Report Version – 2012 (Revised)

Published by:
Northwest Marketing LLC, P. O. Box 3658, Lacey, WA 98509-3658

Power Secret 1:
Do Not Fill Out
Job Applications

I advise clients to avoid filling out job applications because the applications contain so much potentially incriminating and damaging information.

I understand that if you are applying for virtually any public service job (federal, state, county or city position among others), **you will** be required to fill out a job application as part of the hiring process. Just be careful how you answer some key questions, which I am about to share with you.

If you are applying for a private sector job (businesses or organizations), **you may** be required to fill out a job application as part of the hiring process when you are applying for an entry-level job (generally, a minimum wage position up to the supervisory or management level).

Once your reach the supervisory or management level on the employment ladder, it is much more likely that the potential employer will want a resume and cover letter. This is also true of technicians and craftsmen with advanced skills.

It is important that you understand why you have **never been** told the real purpose of why you are asked to fill out an application when applying for a job.

You may not be aware of the fact that the purpose of filling out an application **is not** to qualify you for a job. The real purpose of a job application is to **disqualify** you for a job, and disqualify you in a hurry! That is why applications contain so much incriminating and damaging information, and ask questions that trick you into disqualifying yourself without even knowing you have been had. Here is an example:

While it is illegal to ask you your age, a business can legally ask you your salary history, how much you want to be paid, reasons why you left jobs, your physical ability to perform work functions, and specific references. This information alone is worth much to a business but can **only hurt you**, the client, 99 times out of 100.

Resumes I generate contain none of the aforementioned information. This information is simply not appropriate at the resume stage; it is more appropriate at the interview stage; however, even at the interview stage **it is not appropriate** unless they demonstrate an indicated interest in you as a prospect, and you, in turn, are genuinely interested in the opportunity.

Some clients read an ad in the classifieds online or in a newspaper, and then approach the business (if it is local) with this introduction: "I read your ad for an Administrative Assistant (or whatever the position is) and would like to fill out an application." This approach misses the mark in that it invites filling out an application, which I **do not**, again, recommend.

If you feel you must go to the business to apply, use this language exactly: "I'm interested in your Administrative Assistant (or whatever the job is) position. Here's my resume." Then hand them your resume; it's hard not to take the resume when someone is giving it to you.

They are much more likely to take the resume, peruse it, decide to interview you, and sometimes set an appointment to do so on the spot. On rare occasions, they may even interview you immediately. In any event, you want your resume -- and not an application -- in their hand. Getting your hard copy resume into the hands of the decision-maker -- or at least someone who has input into the decision-making process -- is vital.

Remember, when you fill out an application, **they control the information flow**; they ask the questions (some of which you do not want to answer), and you are obliged to answer. When you are able to give them your resume, **you control the information flow**; you tell them only what you want them to know, and nothing else.

If you think filling out applications can be incriminating and damaging, you are exactly right. Here are two examples, one question that almost always appears on an application, and another that sometimes appears on an application. Both questions are lightening rods that can be a disaster for your future.

The question that almost always appears is: "**Reason for leaving job_____**"

An unthinking potential hire may answer this question by saying any number of damaging responses, including:

"I was only making $12.00 an hour."

"I wanted to work overtime and they wouldn't let me."

"They forced me to work overtime and I needed to pick up my child after school."

"The company was not very reputable. I couldn't trust the management."

"My boss was a micromanager."

"I got absolutely no training, or feedback on how I was doing."

Any or all of these answers **will not** help you, they will hurt your changes of getting hired.

The purpose of this question is to see if you will whine, bitch, moan and complain, giving the impression that you are a difficult person, the kind of person who will bring negative and disruption into the work area.

What you said may be the truth in your mind, but this kind of honest opinion **will not** help you get an offer. You have to be what I call "street smart" about these kinds of situations when trying to get an offer that will lead to getting hired.

When you encounter the question, "Reason for leaving job", always answer it with two words, and **two words only**. Those words are: Better Opportunity.

It could be that the "better opportunity" was that you were making only $12.00 an hour and wanted to make $15.00 an hour, or $20.00 an hour, but do not say or write that as an answer to the question.

It could be that the "better opportunity" was that you wanted to work overtime and they would not let you, or that you did not want to work overtime and they forced you to do so or lose your job. It really doesn't matter what you are unhappy about. You get the point.

If they want to know your last 5 jobs, and you have 5 jobs to list, always answer "better opportunity" to the question, "Reason for leaving job". This will keep you out of trouble, and present a more positive attitude.

On rare occasions, some really sharp interviewer may say to you, "Bill (or whatever you name is), it says here that the reason you left your last 5 jobs was for a better opportunity. What's that about?"

I want you to answer this question by doing 3 things:

1) **Lean forward in your chair**.

2) **Look the interviewer straight in the eye**, and say,

3) "**I thought this was a better opportunity. Was I wrong?**"

This may seem a little bold and audacious (risky), but it puts the ball back in their corner to explain why you should even consider taking their job if they made you an offer. More important, it sets them on notice that they are dealing with a **person of substance**, that you **will not** be pushed around mentally or emotionally.

And, psychologically, what does a person do when you challenge them? They defend themselves and their position. One client of mine used this technique and the interview panel spent their last 20 minutes convincing him why he should take their job offer.

When you show some guts and leadership, people will follow. If you have not noticed, there is never, repeat **never**, a vacuum for followers, whereas there is always a vacuum for leaders. Most people want nothing to do with the responsibility and accountability of being a leader, they are far more comfortable with being a follower. As a follower, they can still use their talents, work very hard to help accomplish a goal, and still not be responsible for its success or failure.

Does it take some self-confidence, a good self-image, and a sense of worth to be bold and audacious? Why, yes, it does, and that is why you should be working on all 3 of these important traits as a potential hire.

The second question on an application that you will see less often is, "**Hobbies and interests____**". Many potential hires would look at this question and think, "What a stupid question. What does this have to do with the price of tea in China? What do my hobbies and interests have to do with this job I am applying for?"

The answer is, "Well, nothing, really." Then you might say, "Why ask the question?" Here's why: Let's say you answer the question by writing, "Flying airplanes, sky diving, motorcycle racing and mountain climbing." What do these activities all have in common? They are dangerous, very dangerous.

Trust me when I say that if you engage in these activities you are tempting fate. The more claims that are made against your company insurance policy, the higher premium (monthly fee) the company will have to pay.

Companies and organizations do not like employees who take chances. It does not matter whether it is flying airplanes, sky diving, motorcycle racing, mountain climbing, drinking, doing drugs, being overweight, or not exercising. Replace these answers with more positive, healthy activities, like walking, hiking, bicycling, jogging or swimming.

When you answer this question on an application, do not say things like collecting guns, target shooting or hunting. Shooting people or animals is not cool, and neither is stepping on ants because you have nothing better to do.

You are also at a disadvantage when you go to a business or organization to fill out an application because many times they want you to do it right then. If you are not well prepared with the information you need to answer specific questions (like dates for jobs from previous years, and mailing addresses of places you worked), then your answers are incomplete, or wrong.

It is really difficult to remember exact dates, times, and places from years ago. Fortunately, much of this distress has been removed in recent years by the advent of the computer age, and filling out applications online. When you apply online in the comfort of your home, you are better able to have access to the information you need.

Many of the major retail businesses today also have computer application systems set up in the store, so you can have more time to respond rather than being under the watchful eye of another person.

I could give a 2-hour seminar on how to fill out applications, but just the knowledge provided here could make your chances at getting an offer 100% better.

Power Secret 2:
Understand The
Most Important Factor
In Writing Resumes

Judgment is the most important factor in writing a resume, and -- as you know, or may not know -- we cannot teach people judgment. We get judgment from life experience, and what experience shows us is that some people simply have better judgment than others. I can show you men who keep running into brick walls because they have not figured out how to climb over them, walk around them, dig under them, or blow them up and walk through. That is a lack of judgment.

If you are a parent, this is what I mean: We raise our children to have a sense of right and wrong, and to make good decisions when it counts. But try as we might, there comes a day and time when we are not there, and someone offers them cigarettes, or drugs, or something worse.

At that point in time, we hope and pray that our child makes the right decision because the wrong decision might lead them down a road from which they may never return. That is judgment. They cannot get it by you simply telling them what to do or not do; they also need modeling, the power of whatever influence you may have with them, and **osmosis**, the gradual or unconscious assimilation of ideas, knowledge and their own life experience.

Judgment is the **most critical factor** you are going to have to come to terms with in writing a resume; or judgment may be your most telling weakness when you go to the street to test its effectiveness. Always remember that it's not just *what* you say, but *how* you say it that counts.

Words have enormous power to trigger positive or negative mental images. Compare the difference, when referring to a young lady or woman by saying "mother" as opposed to saying "unwed mother". These two expressions describing the same woman can make very different impressions.

20

While you may think that the most important information you can give in your resume presentation is your education, your experience, your talents or your particular expertise, how you convey that information can make a world of difference.

If all you have to write about are job descriptions, then you will be in serious trouble. Your job description will be the same job description (work functions) for every other person holding that job worldwide, it will do **absolutely nothing** to separate you from everyone else applying for the same position.

For example, if you are a vice principal at a school, and applying for a principal position, do you really think you are going to educate the superintendent of schools on what a vice principal does on the job?

You should have little or no job description, and instead be sharing your accomplishments and achievements **doing the job** in the same amount of space. Your accomplishments and achievements will in fact separate you from your competition in a hurry. What you do says little (it is, after all, YOUR job, which is no big deal), what you accomplish and achieve says so much more.

Bring something to the table rather than just a job description. What is expected in your job and the consequences of failing at it are of no interest. Focus on your accomplishments.

Always talk about your accomplishments and achievements. Make it easy for the interview panelists to like you, think highly of you, and seriously consider you for a job offer. The easier it is for the powers to be to like you, justify making you an offer, and hire you, the more likely it will happen for you. Do not put hurdles up in front of them, forcing them to jump over the hurdles in order to get to you.

Remember that opportunities to impress are short and can pass quicker than a New York minute. Do I need to remind you that time and tide wait for no man (or woman)?

We say that first impressions are important, and they certainly are. The first impression might also be the last impression, and the only impression.

Power Secret 3:
Be Careful About
From Whom You
Take Your Advice

Always remember that the cheapest commodity in the world is opinions. Everyone has one, and if you do not think so, just ask them; they will tell you. I recommend that you ask a lot of questions and even solicit opinions, but I urge you to be careful about from whom you take your advice. Here is why:

A client makes $100,000 a year, but gets pushed out the door during a merger, acquisition, restructuring or downsizing -- all words for the same negative impact on the person involved, He is upset, heads down to the local watering hole, asks some unemployed, broke person for advice on what to do now, and then listens as if the unemployed, broke person could tell him how to be more financially successful in life. And yet this habit goes on all the time. The sources of advice are all around us: fellow employees, those who did not get axed, other friends, your relative who has never had a job, your pastor, and, if you are desperate enough, your dog Spot.

When you want advice, never go back down the ladder, always climb higher until you reach someone more successful and accomplished than you are in a certain area. **Seek advice from those who are competent through their own experience and success to give advice.**

Always remember that when you take advice from anyone, 999 times out of a 1,000, they **are not** going to be able to hire you. Nor are you going to hire yourself. If you could, you would be self-employed, which is not always saying a lot.

If you trade hours for dollars in a work-a-day job, you are employed, you **have a job**. When you decide to go into business for yourself and become self-employed, you may just **own a job**. There are countless self-employed people who work far harder and longer than people who have a job, and yet make less money, have less benefits, and have more stress and worry than those who trade hours for dollars. Be careful in getting and taking advice.

22

Power Secret 4:
Why You Will
Not Be Able
To Relate To Everyone

I tell clients that for every 10 people who could potentially make the decision to interview you or hire you, 3 out of the 10 will like you, and it will have nothing to do with what you do.

They may simply **like** your smile, your handshake, the sound of your voice, or the way you part your hair.

Rest assured that 3 out of those same 10 people will not like you, and again it will have nothing to do with what you do.

They may simply **not like** your smile, your handshake, the sound of your voice, or the way you part your hair.

Four out of those same 10 people will learn to like you or dislike you as they develop a working relationship with you. The odds say that those 4 in 10 will like you if you work at earning their respect, honor their confidence, and treat them as you would want to be treated.

Considering these numbers, you should be able to develop a very good working relationship with about 70% of your fellow employees when you are hired, and go to work.

The other 30% you can forget, and if you bend over backwards to cultivate their good will, you will usually find that they always have a reason to whine or complain about what is happening to them, and why the world is not treating them right. They are, in a word, negative. **Your best positive will not likely overcome their worst negative.** So forget about them, or they may do mental harm to your psyche.

Why do people like or not like you based upon things that really have little to do with your skills and abilities?

The answer is simply that people are most often more emotional than rational. People are filled up with prejudices, beliefs, foibles and idiosyncrasies. They will continually tell you that cat is spelled "kat" even though you would lead them to a dictionary, and show them that cat is spelled "cat".

A man convinced against his will is of the same opinion still.

A woman convinced against her will is of the same opinion still.

Under the category of "people are not always rational" is also the phenomenon of "life is not always fair".

For those of us who have been paying attention, life **is not** fair, and it is not just an occasional circumstance that arises.

A good example of this would be a client named Karen who went to a job interview, had a fantastic experience at the interview, came away feeling good about herself, and her prospects of being hired.

She knew that the company representatives liked her and would offer her a job. She did not get the offer. Later she learned that everyone liked her, but the key decision-maker axed her hiring, even though he seemed to have liked her at the interview.

What Karen did not know was that the key decision-maker was going through a nasty divorce and child custody battle, and his ex-wife's name was Karen. He simply did not want to come to work every day and have to smile at this Karen and say, "Good morning, Karen, how are you doing?" Such is life.

So get over taking every negative thing that happens to you personally. This is **not always** about you, it is about other people and their perceptions of you. In more cases than not, it has nothing to do with you.

Someone else may get the job offer rather than you. Understand that **50%** of all people who are hired or promoted are not the most qualified candidates.

And **60%** of all people who are hired or promoted involve some degree of influence. Do not get angry and upset.

The person who is hired or promoted may be just as qualified, or more qualified, than you are – they just simply know someone who has influence, or someone who has influence may know them and want to help them. Here is the lesson to be learned: **Meet and make friends** because you never know when they may become aware of an opportunity, know that you are looking, and pass on the lead to you.

You could, and should, **network like the world ends tomorrow**, and there is a chance that you can go to heaven, but you need 100 good people to vouch for you before St. Peter at the Pearly Gates.

Seriously, do not put off networking. With the advent of social networking today (Facebook, Twitter, LinkedIn, and MySpace to name a few), it is easier to create more and more contacts faster. We can debate about the effectiveness of doing so, but research suggests that doing so is a good idea, if for no other reason than people like to help people they know, like and trust.

Fundamentally, the same thing is true in sales. Smart, successful sales people know that people really only buy for two reasons. Complete this sentence:

Said simply, people buy from people they (what). The answer is, people buy from people they

    1) **like**, or

    2) **trust**.

Period. That's it. People buy from people they like, or they buy from people they trust.

The same is true for people who recommend other people for jobs. They like the person they recommend and/or they trust the person they recommend. After all, they do not want to be embarrassed by the people they recommend, and, if they do not like you or trust you, they are not going to put their reputation on the line recommending you.

You become a reflection on them through association. Both the person recommending and the person recommended have something to gain or to lose.

People without friends and contacts **are helpless** to help themselves by influence. Therefore, it behooves you to meet and make as many friends and contacts as you can.

Power Secret 5:
How To Make Money
Without A College Degree

It is worth pointing out that many times there is no **meaningful** correlation between education and income.

One can statistically show that a college graduate, over the course of his or her adult working life, will make more money than a high school graduate who does not go on to higher education.

The problem is that many times the difference between the two is not that great of a difference. It is not like **all** college graduates make an average of $100,000 a year and **all** high school graduates make an average of only $30,000 a year.

I understand that if you are a doctor or an attorney, well placed and competent, you are going to make a potentially huge income compared to people who do not have a medical or juris doctor degree -- a professional degree that potentially leads to a much larger annual income. But what about all of the college graduates without professional degrees who end up at McDonald's while they are trying to find a challenging, good paying position that interests them?

Clearly, without a college degree that leads to a high paying profession, you cannot expect to knock down the big bucks.

Some clients come to me with a bachelor's degree, have been out of school for 10 years, and are making less than $35,000 a year. You are going to have a hard time convincing them that a college education has put them on easy street. The reason they are making only $35,000 a year is not because they are underpaid; it is more likely because they are underemployed.

Clients in this position generally do not have an education problem, a training problem, an intelligence problem, or a refusal to work problem. They usually have a marketing problem. **They simply do not know how to market themselves.**

Just as many times there is no meaningful correlation between education and income, so is there no meaningful correlation between intelligence and income. There are educated idiots everywhere. A high I.Q. does not automatically equate to a high income.

An intelligence quotient simply means you have ability to learn things quickly; it does not necessarily follow that you have the ability to retain what you learn, and even more important, the ability to apply the information you retain. Slow learners who have the ability to retain and apply information, can substantially out earn people with a high I.Q.

Many times there is also no meaningful correlation between talent and income. Have you ever heard of the proverbial starving artist? How many talented actors have gone to Hollywood and, like thousands of others, not been discovered?

How can we then explain why I have clients who earn more than $200,000 in annual income and do so with a high school degree and sometimes even without a high school degree? I have one client who earns $400,000 annually and is a high school dropout.

The answer is that you can show a meaningful correlation between people skills and income.

In almost every case, if you show me a person who is not in a high paying profession, does not have a college degree, and makes $200,000 plus a year, I will show you a person with obvious people skills.

I have personally helped more than 5,400 clients get a job, or get a better job. And the vast majority of those clients are either educated with a degree or degrees, literate, have good paying positions ($60,000 and up), and already have a good job title (manager, supervisor or technician). In other words, I have been in the high-end of the resume writing business.

I can help anyone who wants to take the time and trouble to listen and apply the tactics, techniques and procedures I recommend at every stage of the job-hiring process. I am in the high-end of the resume writing business because the people who are willing to do these things already have good jobs and good futures – that is how they got where they are -- they acted in their best self-interest, and reaped the results of their efforts. When they come to me, they simply know they can earn more, and want to earn more money.

Bonus Power Secret 6: What To Do When It Does Not Work For You

This is the Protestant ethic: work hard, keep your nose clean, and good things will happen. Too often today, good things do not happen, which might explain why a lot of folks have little use for the Protestant ethic.

How many times have you seen a fellow employee who was hired or promoted, but who was not really the most qualified person to be hired or promoted?

Yes, you're seething too. Someone might say: "I can't believe they hired that person", or "I can't believe they promoted that jerk. If they only knew."

The fact is, that again, **more than 50% of the time, the person hired or promoted is not the most qualified.**

It is really simple. People who hire get a lot of pressure to go through all their relatives, friends, neighbors and lovers to find prospects to hire or promote.

Granted that much of this occurs at entry level to mid-management positions, but it occurs **none the less.**

I do have some good news for you: the people who get hired or promoted are oftentimes not the most qualified, but many times they have done the best job of presenting what it is they have to offer.

This means that many, many clients who are not the most qualified can also get hired or promoted if they do the best job of presenting what it is they have to offer, and that is exactly what you need to do: **the best possible job of presenting what it is that you have to offer.**

28

It is all the more reason you need to learn and use the tools, tactics and procedures that will help you get ahead faster.

Check out my websites:

1) Quality Resumes by Ed Bagley
at: http://quality-resumes-by-ed-bagley.com

Offers Quality Resume Writing and Job Counseling Services with Ed Bagley and His Time, Talent, Experience and Expertise in Helping Market Potential Hires. Ed Works With You Personally. An Author and Professional Writer, Ed Has 25+ Years of Experience and Has Helped 5,400+ Clients Acquire New Jobs.

2) Ed Bagley's Blog
at: http://www.edbagleyblog.com

Ed Bagley's Blog with his news, coverage and commentary as a writer, author, newspaper publisher and book publisher during the past 50 years.

3) Ed Bagley's Blog Archives
at: http://ed-bagley-blog-archives.com

Ed Bagley's Blog Archives has his first 971 original articles on 54 different subjects covering 69,000+ pages, including coverage on college football, college basketball, track, distance running, movies, business, marketing, family, relationships, life, faith and politics. Did I forget to mention humor?

4) Ed Bagley's College Football
at: http://ed-bagley-college-football.com

A Single Subject Website on the Current and Past NCAA College Football Seasons That Has a 14-Week Wrap-Up of the Major College Action, Complete Annual Bowl Game Coverage, and the Annual National Championship Game.

5) Northwest Marketing LLC
at: http://northwest-marketing.com

Northwest Marketing LLC is the parent company of several websites, including Quality Resumes by Ed Bagley, Ed Bagley's Bog, Ed Bagley's Blog Archives, Ed Bagley's College Football, Inside a Job Interview, and How to Write a Single Page Resume.

19021318R00018

Made in the USA
Charleston, SC
03 May 2013